Karen Jacobs' Sargent Choice Test Kitchen: 10th Anniversary

A Nutrition & Occupational Therapy Collaboration

Designed by Megan Bartley
Illustrated by Katie Hay

Copyright © 2019 Karen Jacobs

ISBN: 978-0-9982119-5-4

All rights reserved. This book or any portion thereof may not be reproduced or used in any manner whatsoever without the express written permission of the publisher except for the use of brief quotations in a book review or scholarly journal.

Library of Congress Control Number: 2019914110

Printed in the United States of America

Acknowledgements

To my family. Mom and Dad, thank you for always believing in me, no matter how big my dreams are. Mom and grandmas, thank you for cultivating my love of baking over the years.

To my friends. Near or far, thank you for making this world a better place, and for helping me become the person I am today.

To my best friend, Katie Hay, thank you for all of the kitchen karaoke and for illustrating this cookbook. I'm so grateful we get to do life together.

To Karen Jacobs. Thank you for inviting me into this project and for your dedication to your friends and students.

Finally, thank you to the One who makes dreams come true. *Megan*

Many thanks to Jennifer Culbert, the Sargent Choice Nutrition Center, and the Sargent Choice Ambassadors for their dedication and commitment to the Sargent Choice Test Kitchen; and to all the students who have joined us in learning to cook and make healthy Sargent Choice recipes. It has been a joy to work with all of you. Finally, to Megan who made this 10 year celebration of recipes a reality. *Karen*

Table of Contents

2-3	Southwestern Corn and Black Bean Salad
4-5	Brown Rice Sushi
6-7	Oven-Baked Vegetable Burritos with Cheese
8-9	Black Bean Burgers
10-11	Caramelized Onion and Goat Cheese Pizza
12-13	Spicy Lentils with Sweet Potatoes and Kale
14-15	Roasted Root Vegetables with Rosemary
16-17	Karen's Beloved Potato Latkes
18-19	Kale and White Bean Potpie with Chive Biscuits
20-21	Shredded Jackfruit Burritos
24-25	Pumpkin Cranberry Muffins
26-27	Whole Grain Peanut Butter Chocolate Chip Cookies
28-29	Autumn Coffee Cake
30-31	Mocha Cupcakes with Mocha Cream Cheese Frosting
32-33	Mini Cheesecakes
34-35	Biscotti
36-37	Fudgy Black Bean Brownies
38-39	Blueberry Lemon Yogurt Cake
40-41	Blueberry Baked Oatmeal
42-43	Mug Cakes

Tips and Tricks

COMMON MEASUREMENT CONVERSIONS

1 Tablespoon = 3 teaspoons
4 Tablespoons = ¼ cup
¼ cup = 2 ounces (oz)
½ cup = 4 ounces (oz)
¾ cup = 6 ounces (oz)
1 cup = 8 ounces (oz)

DRY VS. LIQUID MEASURING CUPS

This cookbook has dry and liquid measuring cups in the tools for the recipes. They hold the same amount of an item. The difference is how easy it is to measure. Liquid measuring cups make it easier to measure wet items. Dry measuring cups make it easier to measure dry items. To successfully make these recipes, you do not need to have both.

savory

2009
Southwestern Corn and Black Bean Salad

Tools

 Stovetop	 Skillet	 Utensils	 Large Bowl	 Cutting Board	 Knives
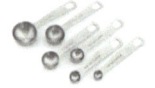 Measuring Spoons	 Dry & Liquid Measuring Cups		 Refrigerator		 Strainer

Ingredients

 10 ounces frozen corn	 ½ cup pine nuts	 ¼ cup lime juice	 2 Tbsp olive oil	 ¼ cup cilantro	 ½ tsp salt	 ¼ tsp pepper
 30 ounces black beans	 2 cups red cabbage		 1 large orange bell pepper		 2 large tomatoes	 ¼ cup red onion

Directions

STEP 1: Dry Measuring Cups; Stovetop; Skillet; Wooden Spoon

Place the pine nuts in a small dry skillet over medium-low heat. Cook for 2-4 minutes until lightly browned. Stir with spoon to prevent burning.

STEP 2: Cutting Board; Knives; Large Bowl; Whisk; Dry Measuring Cups; Measuring Spoons

Chop the cilantro. Add cilantro, lime juice, olive oil, salt, and pepper into a large bowl. Whisk until combined.

STEP 3: Strainer; Cutting Board; Knives; Dry Measuring Cups

Thoroughly drain and rinse the black beans. Shred the red cabbage. Dice the orange bell pepper and tomatoes. Mince the red onion.

STEP 4: Large Bowl; Spoon; Refrigerator

Add the corn, pine nuts, beans, cabbage, tomato, onion, and bell pepper to the large bowl. Stir with the spoon. Refrigerate until ready to serve.

STEP 5:

Optional Serve with tortilla chips.

2010
Brown Rice Sushi

Tools

 Spoons	 Stovetop	 Cutting Knives	 Cutting Board	 Bowls	 Medium Pot
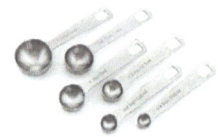 Measuring Spoons	 Peeler	 Water	 Sushi Mat	 Dry & Liquid Measuring Cup	

Ingredients

 ⅔ cup dry brown rice	 1 cup + 1 tsp water	 2 tsp soy sauce	 2 Tbsp rice vinegar	 1 tsp wasabi powder	 ½ cucumber
 ½ carrot	 ½ avocado	 ¾ ounces radish sprouts	 6 ounces firm tofu	 2 (8 ¼ x 7 ¼ in.) roasted nori	

	Directions	

STEP 1: Cutting Board; Knives; Peeler

Wash cucumber, carrot, avocado, and radish sprouts. Cucumber: Peel, cut in half, take out the seeds, and cut into 1/16th inch-thick sticks. Carrot: Cut in half, then cut into 1/16th inch-thick sticks. Avocado: Cut in half, then peel and cut into thin slices. Radish sprouts: trim off the roots. Tofu: Cut into several long pieces.

STEP 2: Liquid Measuring Cup; Measuring Spoons; Medium Pot; Wooden Spoon; Stovetop

Put 1 cup of water in the pot. Bring to boil. Put rice and 1 tsp soy sauce in boiling water. Stir with large spoon for 5 seconds. Cook for 10-15 minutes. Turn off stovetop.

STEP 3: Small Bowl; Large Bowl; Wooden Spoon; Measuring Spoons

In a small bowl, stir together vinegar and 1 tsp soy sauce. Transfer rice to large bowl. Pour the vinegar mixture over rice. Stir with large spoon. Let cool for 15 minutes.

STEP 4: Small Bowl; Small Spoon; Measuring Spoons

In a small bowl, stir together wasabi powder and 1 tsp of water to form a stiff paste.

STEP 6: Sushi Mat; Bowl of Water; Cutting Board; Knives

Assembly: Place 1 sheet of nori lengthwise shiny side down on sushi mat. Dip fingers in the bowl of water. Gently press half of the rice onto the nori with a 1 ¾-inch border on the farthest edge. Arrange half of the cucumber, carrot, avocado, radish sprouts, and tofu pieces in an even strip horizontally across the rice (cut if needed). Roll the bottom edge of mat toward the top edge while firmly holding the filling in place. Press firmly to seal the roll. Let stand for five minutes. Cut crosswise into 6 pieces with a wet knife. Repeat with the second sheet of nori.

2011
Oven-Baked Vegetable Burritos with Cheese

Tools

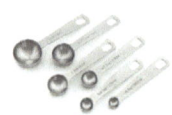 Measuring Spoons	 Dry & Liquid Measuring Cups	 Stovetop & Oven	 Potholders
 Utensils	 Knives	 Cutting Board	 Small Bowl	 Large Skillet	 9x13" Baking Dish	 Aluminum Foil

Ingredients

 2 cups onion	 4 cloves garlic	 4 fresh jalapeno peppers	 2 Tbsp. olive oil	 4 tomatoes	 1 ½ cup zucchini	 2 tsp. cumin
 1 ½ cup summer squash	 1 pound black beans	 1 pound pinto beans	 1 cup tomato sauce	 1 tsp. pepper	1 cup Monterey Jack cheese	 6 10-in. wheat wraps

Directions

STEP 1: Oven

Preheat oven to 350°F.

STEP 2: Cutting Board; Knives; Dry Measuring Cups

Chop the onion, jalapeño peppers, tomatoes, zucchini, and summer squash.

STEP 3: Stovetop; Skillet; Spoon

In the skillet, cook the onion, garlic, and jalapeno peppers, until the onion is softened. Stir often. Add the tomato, zucchini, and summer squash. Cook until all of the vegetables are soft.

STEP 4: Small Bowl; Fork

Put half of the black beans and pinto beans in the small bowl. Mash them with the fork. Add all of the black beans and pinto beans into the skillet.

STEP 5: Liquid Measuring Cup; Measuring Spoons

Add the tomato sauce, cumin, and pepper into the skillet. Bring to a slow simmer for 3-5 minutes until slightly thickened.

STEP 6: Spoon; Baking Dish; Aluminum Foil

Spread a spoonful of the filling and some cheese into each wrap. Keep the ends open while you roll it closed. Arrange burritos seam down in a baking dish. Put the remaining cheese on top. Cover with foil and bake in the oven for 20 minutes.

STEP 7: Oven; Potholders; Spoon

Use potholders to remove pan from oven. Set on the top of the stove. Turn oven off. Serve burritos warm.

2012
Black Bean Burgers

Tools

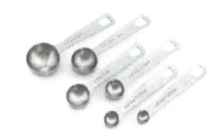 Measuring Spoons	 Dry Measuring Cups	 Stovetop	 Utensils	 Knives
 Cutting Board	 Small & Large Bowl	 Large Skillet	 Peeler	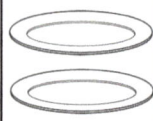 Plates

Ingredients

 1 can (15 oz) unsalted black beans	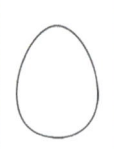 1 egg	 ½ onion	 1 cup whole wheat bread crumbs	 ½ tsp garlic powder	 ½ jalapeño
 ½ red pepper	 1-2 Tbsp olive oil	 to taste salt & pepper	 4 whole-wheat hamburger buns	 1 avocado	 1-2 tsp lime juice

Directions

STEP 1: Cutting board; Knives; Dry Measuring Cups

BURGERS: Chop <u>onion</u>, <u>jalapeno</u>, <u>red pepper</u>.

STEP 2: Large Bowl; Fork; Measuring Spoons

Put <u>black beans</u> in a large bowl and mash well with a fork. Add <u>egg</u>, <u>onion</u>, <u>bread crumbs</u>, <u>garlic powder</u>, <u>jalapeno</u>, <u>red pepper</u>, <u>salt</u>, and <u>pepper</u>. Mix well to combine. Shape mixture into 6 round patties and place on 1 plate.

STEP 3 Stovetop; Skillet; Spatula

Heat <u>oil</u> in a large skillet over medium heat. Arrange patties in a single layer and cook for 5 minutes. Flip patty and cook for 5 more minutes. Place on <u>hamburger bun</u> or plate. Turn stovetop off.

STEP 4: Peeler; Knife; Fork; Small Bowl; Measuring Spoons

GUACAMOLE: Peel and mash the <u>avocado</u> in a small bowl. Add the <u>lime juice</u> and <u>garlic powder</u>. Season with <u>salt</u> and <u>pepper</u> to taste. Mix well. Add to burger.

2013
Caramelized Onion and Goat Cheese Pizza

Tools

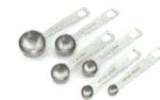 Measuring Spoon	  Dry & Liquid Measuring Cups	 Stovetop & Oven	 Potholders
 Utensils	 Knives	 Cutting Board	 Large Skillet with Lid	 Baking Sheet	 Small Bowl

Ingredients

 2 tsp. olive oil	 2 cups onion	 1 prepared wheat pizza dough	 for dusting work surface wheat flour
 ½ cup tomato sauce	 ¼ cup fresh basil	 ¼ cup sun-dried tomato halves	 ⅔ cup (3 oz) goat cheese

Directions

STEP 1: Oven

Preheat oven to 450ºF.

STEP 3: Cutting Board; Knives; Measuring Cups

Chop onion, sun-dried tomatoes, and fresh basil.

STEP 4: Stovetop; Large Skillet with Lid; Spoon

Heat olive oil in the skillet over medium-high heat. Add onion; cover with lid and cook for 3 minutes. Take off the lid and cool for 11 more minutes. Stir often.

STEP 5: Baking Sheet; Oven; Potholders

Stretch the dough into a 12 inch circle on a lightly floured baking sheet. Place in oven for 5 minutes. Use potholders to remove prepared wheat pizza crust.

STEP 6: Small Bowl; Spoon; Liquid Measuring Cup

Combine tomato sauce and sun-dried tomatoes in small bowl. Spread the sauce mixture over pre-baked wheat pizza crust. Top with onion and goat cheese.

STEP 7: Oven; Potholders; Pizza Cutter

Bake for 10 minutes. Remove pizza and set on stovetop. Sprinkle with fresh basil. Cut into 6 slices. Turn oven off.

2014
Spicy Lentils with Sweet Potatoes and Kale

Tools

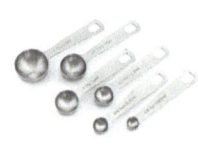 Measuring Spoons	 Dry & Liquid Measuring Cup	 Stovetop	 Spoon
 Medium Pot	 Cutting Board	 Knives	 Peeler

Ingredients

 2 tsp canola oil	 ¼ cup onion	 1 stalk celery	 1 carrot	 1 sweet potato	 1 tsp minced garlic	 1 bunch kale
 ½ cup green lentils	 1 bay leaf	 2 sprigs rosemary	 1 whole serrano pepper		 ¼ tsp salt	 2 cups vegetable stock

Directions

STEP 1: Peeler; Cutting Board; Knives; Dry Measuring Cups

Peel carrot and sweet potato. Dice onion, celery, carrot, and sweet potato.

STEP 2: Measuring Spoons; Medium Pot; Stovetop; Spoon

Heat oil in medium pot. Once oil is hot, add onion, celery, carrot, and sweet potato. Cook for 6 minutes. Add minced garlic and kale. Cook until kale wilts.

STEP 3: Stovetop; Spoon; Measuring Spoons

Add green lentils, bay leaf, rosemary sprigs, whole serrano pepper, and vegetable stock. Bring to boil. Turn down the heat. Cook for 30 minutes. Turn stovetop off. Add salt. Stir well.

STEP 4: Spoon

Before serving, remove bay leaf, serrano pepper, and rosemary sprigs.

2015
Roasted Root Vegetables with Rosemary

Tools

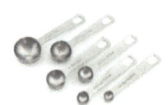 Measuring Spoons	 Liquid Measuring Cup	 Oven	 Potholders	 Spoon
 Cutting Board	 Very Large Bowl	 Knives	 Baking Sheets	 Peeler

Ingredients

 cooking spray	 1 pound red potatoes	 1 pound celery root	 1 pound turnips	 1 pound carrots	 1 pound parsnips
 2 onions	 2 leeks	 2 Tbsp rosemary	 1 tsp salt	 pepper (to taste)	 ⅓ cup olive oil	 10 garlic cloves

Directions

STEP 1: Oven

Position 1 rack in the center of oven and 1 rack in the bottom 1/3 of oven. Preheat to 400ºF.

STEP 3: Baking Sheets

Spray both baking sheets with cooking spray.

STEP 4: Cutting Board; Knives; Peeler

Wash red potatoes. Peel celery root, turnips, carrots, parsnips, and garlic. Dice potatoes, celery root, turnips, carrots, parsnips, onions, and leeks into 1-inch pieces. Chop rosemary.

STEP 5: Very Large Bowl; Measuring Spoons; Liquid Measuring Cup; Spoon; Oven

Add all ingredients EXCEPT garlic to bowl. Mix well. Divide mixture between baking sheets. Place 1 sheet on each oven rack. Roast for 30 minutes. Stir often.

STEP 6: Potholders; Spoon

Add 5 garlic cloves to each baking sheet. Switch pans onto different oven racks. Bake 35 minutes. Remove from oven, transfer to large bowl. Turn oven off. Serve hot.

2016
Karen's Beloved Potato Latkes

Tools

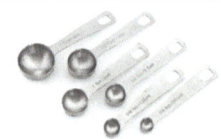 Measuring Spoons	 Dry Measuring Cups	 Stovetop	 Utensils

 Cutting Board	 Bowl	 Knives	 Large Skillet	 Peeler	 Grater	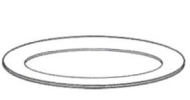 Warm Plate

Ingredients

 4 sweet potatoes	 1 cup onion	 ½ cup wheat flour	Garnish:  2 cups unsweetened applesauce
 4 Tbsp olive oil	 ⅛ tsp pepper	 4 eggs	

Directions

STEP 1: Cutting Board; Knives; Peeler; Grater; Dry Measuring Cups

Dice onion. Peel and grate sweet potatoes.

STEP 3: Bowl; Fork; Spoon; Dry Measuring Cups; Measuring Spoons

Lightly beat eggs in the bowl with the fork. Add sweet potatoes, onion, and pepper. Stir well to combine. Add wheat flour. Mix again. (Only add enough flour to make a batter – not too dry or too stiff.)

STEP 4: Measuring Spoons; Large Skillet; Stovetop; Spoon; Spatula; Warm Plate

Heat half of the olive oil over medium-high heat in skillet. Drop large spoonfuls of batter into skillet. Press gently with spatula to flatten batter. Fry 4 to 5 minutes until brown. Flip and cook 3 to 4 more minutes. Remove latkes to warm plate. Repeat process with remaining oil and batter. Turn stovetop off.

STEP 5:

Serve immediately with applesauce.

2017
Kale and White Bean Potpie with Chive Biscuits

Tools

 Measuring Spoons	Dry & Liquid Measuring Cup	Stovetop & Oven	 Potholders
Utensils	Knives	Bowl	Cutting Board	Strainer	Large Pot	2-quart Baking Dish

Ingredients : Kale Soup

 cooking spray	 2 ½ Tbsp olive oil	 1 cup onion	 ½ cup carrot	 ½ cup celery	 3 tsp minced garlic	 2 tsp thyme
 1 tsp rosemary	 8 cups kale	 ¼ cup wheat flour	 3 cups vegetable broth	 1 can (15 oz) white beans	 ½ tsp salt & pepper	

18

Ingredients : Chive Biscuits

 1 cup wheat flour	1 tsp baking powder	¼ tsp baking soda	 ¼ tsp salt & pepper	 3 Tbsp cold butter	 3 Tbsp fresh chives	 ½ cup cold buttermilk

Directions

STEP 1: Oven; Baking Dish

Preheat oven to 350°F. Spray baking dish with <u>cooking spray</u>.

STEP 2: Cutting Board; Knives; Dry Measuring Cups; Measuring Spoons; Strainer

Chop <u>onion</u>, <u>carrot</u>, <u>celery</u>, <u>thyme</u>, <u>rosemary</u>, and <u>kale</u>. Strain <u>white beans</u>. Rinse.

STEP 3: Measuring Spoons; Liquid Measuring Cup; Large Pot; Stovetop; Spoon

Heat 2 Tbsp <u>oil</u> in large pot over medium heat. Add <u>onion</u>, <u>carrot</u>, <u>celery</u> to large pot. Cook 4 to 6 minutes. Add <u>minced garlic</u>, <u>thyme</u>, and <u>rosemary</u>. Stir for 30 seconds. Add <u>kale</u>. Stir. Cook for 3 to 5 minutes. Sprinkle with ¼ cup <u>wheat flour</u>. Stir for 30 seconds. Stir in <u>vegetable broth</u>. Increase to high heat and bring to a boil. Reduce heat to simmer, stir and cook for 2 minutes. Stir in <u>white beans</u>, <u>salt</u>, and <u>pepper</u>. Transfer to prepared pan. Turn stovetop off.

STEP 4 – Chive Biscuits: Cutting Board; Knives; Measuring Spoons; Bowl; Whisk; Spoon; Oven; Potholders

Chop <u>chives</u>. Whisk 1 cup <u>wheat flour</u>, <u>baking powder</u>, <u>baking soda</u>, <u>salt</u>, and <u>pepper</u> in a bowl. Use fingers to rub <u>butter</u> into dry ingredients. Stir in <u>chives</u>. Add <u>buttermilk</u>. Stir until just combined. Form dough into 6 biscuits. Place on top of vegetable mixture. Place in oven. Bake 30 minutes (until filling is bubbling). Turn oven off.

2018
Shredded Jackfruit Burritos

Tools

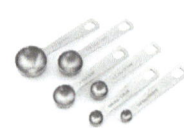 Measuring Spoons	 Liquid Measuring Cup	 Wooden Spoon

 Cutting Board	 Knives	 Stovetop	 Large Skillet

Ingredients

 1 can (20 oz) green jackfruit	 1 Tbsp olive oil	 1 onion	4 tsp minced garlic	 1 tsp paprika	 1 ½ tsp chili powder

 ½ cup water	1 Tbsp lime juice	½ tsp salt	 6 small wheat wraps

Other Filling Options:	brown rice shredded cabbage salsa black beans

Directions

STEP 1: Cutting Board; Knives

Chop <u>onion</u>.

STEP 2: Measuring Spoons; Liquid Measuring Cup; Large Skillet; Stovetop; Spoon

Heat <u>oil</u> in large skillet over medium-high heat. Stir in <u>onion</u>. Sauté for 5 minutes. Stir in <u>garlic</u>, <u>paprika</u>, and <u>chili powder</u>. Add <u>water</u>, <u>lime juice</u>, <u>salt</u>, and <u>drained jackfruit</u>. Cook for 5 to 10 minutes until most of the liquid is absorbed. Use spoon to smash <u>jackfruit</u> (this creates a shredded texture). Turn stovetop off.

STEP 3:

Put <u>jackfruit</u> and other <u>fillings</u> in an open-faced <u>wheat wrap</u>. Fold in the sides and roll.

Sweet

2009
Pumpkin Cranberry Muffins

Tools

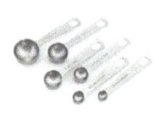 Measuring Spoons	  Dry & Liquid Measuring Cup	 Oven	 Potholders	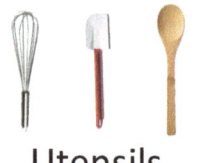 Utensils
 Large Bowls	  Muffin Tins	 Muffin Cup Liners	 Toothpick	 Cooling Rack

Ingredients

 1 ½ cups wheat flour	 1 tsp baking soda	 ¾ cup sugar	 ¾ tsp ginger	 ½ tsp cinnamon	 ½ cup buttermilk	 ¼ tsp salt
 ¼ cup light brown sugar	 ½ tsp baking powder	 1 cup pumpkin	 ⅛ tsp cloves	 2 Tbsp canola oil	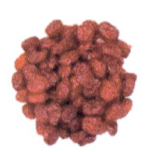 ⅔ cup dried cranberries	 1 egg

Directions

STEP 1: Oven

Preheat oven to 375°F.

STEP 2: Muffin Tins; Muffin Cup Liners

Place 12 muffin cup liners in muffin tin.

STEP 3: Large Bowl; Whisk; Dry Measuring Cups; Measuring Spoons

Combine <u>wheat flour</u>, <u>baking soda</u>, <u>baking powder</u>, <u>ginger</u>, <u>cinnamon</u>, <u>cloves</u>, and <u>salt</u> into a bowl. Whisk together.

STEP 4: Large Bowl; Dry Measuring Cups; Liquid Measuring Cup

Combine <u>sugar</u>, <u>brown sugar</u>, <u>pumpkin</u>, <u>oil</u>, <u>buttermilk</u>, and <u>egg</u> in another bowl. Whisk for 5 minutes. Add <u>flour mixture</u> to <u>sugar mixture</u>. Mix until combined. Fold in <u>cranberries</u>.

STEP 5: Muffin Tins; Spoon; Oven; Toothpick; Potholders; Cooling Rack

Spoon batter into muffin tin. Bake for 25 minutes. Check with toothpick. Remove muffins from pan. Place on cooling rack. Turn oven off.

2010
Whole Grain Peanut Butter Chocolate Chip Cookies

Tools

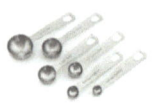 Measuring Spoons	  Dry & Liquid Measuring Cups	 Oven	 Potholders
 Utensils	 Electric Mixer	 Bowls	 Baking Sheets	 Cooling Rack

Ingredients

 1 cup wheat flour	 1 ¼ cup quick oats	 1 tsp baking soda	 ½ tsp salt	 ½ cup peanut butter	 ⅔ cup mini chocolate chips
 ⅜ cup light brown sugar	 ⅜ cup sugar	 ½ cup canola oil	 2 eggs	 1 tsp vanilla	 1 cup chopped nuts

Directions

STEP 1: Oven

Preheat oven to 350°F.

STEP 2: Small and Large Bowls; Spoon; Electric Mixer; Dry and Liquid Measuring Cups; Measuring Spoons

Small bowl - Combine <u>wheat flour</u>, <u>oats</u>, <u>baking soda</u>, and <u>salt</u>. Mix with spoon. These are the <u>dry ingredients.</u> Large bowl – beat <u>oil</u>, <u>peanut butter</u>, <u>sugar</u>, <u>brown sugar</u>, and <u>vanilla</u> with electric mixer. These are the <u>wet ingredients.</u>

STEP 3:

Add <u>eggs</u> into <u>wet ingredients</u>. Mix well. Slowly add the <u>dry ingredients</u> to the <u>wet ingredients</u>. Mix with electric mixer. Fold in <u>chocolate chips</u> and <u>nuts</u> with rubber spatula.

STEP 4: Spoon; Baking Sheets; Oven; Potholders; Cooling Rack

Drop large spoonfuls of dough onto baking sheet. Bake for 8 to 10 minutes. Cool on baking sheets for 2 minutes, then remove to cooling rack. Turn oven off.

2011 Autumn Coffee Cake

Tools

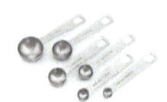 Measuring Spoons	 Dry & Liquid Measuring Cup	 Oven	 Potholders	 Utensils	 Bowls
 Peeler	 9X13 Baking Dish	 Grater	 Toothpick		 Cooling Rack

Ingredients

 ⅔ cup canola oil	 ¼ tsp salt	2 tsp cinnamon	1 ½ cups buttermilk	 1 ½ cups carrots	1 cup apples	2 eggs
 1 ¾ cups rolled oats	 1 ½ cups wheat flour	 ¼ cup ground flaxseed	 1 Tbsp baking soda	1 tsp baking powder		1 cup light brown sugar
Topping:	 1/3 cup wheat flour	 ¼ cup oats	2 Tbsp light brown sugar	1 tsp cinnamon		 2 Tbsp canola oil

Directions

STEP 1: Oven; Baking Dish

Position an oven rack in the center of the oven. Preheat oven to 350°F. Spray the baking dish.

STEP 2: Peeler; Grater

Peel carrots and apples. Grate carrots and apples.

STEP 3: Medium Bowl; Spoon; Dry Measuring Cups; Measuring Spoons

Add oats, flour, flaxseeds, baking soda, baking powder, cinnamon, and salt in medium bowl. Stir to combine.

STEP 4: Large Bowl; Whisk; Liquid Measuring Cup; Dry Measuring Cups

Whisk together brown sugar and oil. Add eggs and beat well. Stir in buttermilk.

STEP 5: Baking Dish

Add oat mixture to buttermilk mixture. Stir well. Add carrots and apples. Stir until combined. Transfer batter to baking dish.

STEP 6: Small Bowl; Spoon

Topping – Add flour, oats, brown sugar, cinnamon, and oil in small bowl. Stir to blend. Sprinkle evenly on top of batter.

STEP 7: Oven; Potholders; Toothpick; Cooling Rack

Bake for 45 minutes. Check with toothpick. Turn oven off. Let cool on cooling rack for 1 hour. Cut into 24 pieces.

2012
Mocha Cupcakes with Mocha Cream Cheese Frosting

Tools

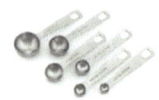 Measuring Spoons	 Dry & Liquid Measuring Cup	 Oven	 Potholders	 Utensils	 Electric Mixer
 Bowls	 Muffin Tins	 Muffin Cup Liners	 Microwave	 Toothpick	 Cooling Rack

Ingredients

 1 ¼ cup wheat flour	 ½ cup cocoa powder	 ¼ tsp salt	 1 tsp baking soda	 1 tsp baking powder	 2 Tbsp butter
 1 Tbsp canola oil	1 tsp powdered coffee	2 eggs + 2 egg whites	1 ½ cups nonfat yogurt	3 tsp vanilla	¾ cup sugar
 2 oz dark chocolate	 8 oz cream cheese	1/3 cup powdered sugar		 1 tsp powdered coffee	1 tsp vanilla

Directions

STEP 1: Oven; Muffin Tins and Liners

Preheat oven to 350°F. Put muffin cup liners in muffin tin.

STEP 2: Whisk; Medium Bowl; Dry Measuring Cups; Measuring Spoons

Whisk together flour, cocoa, salt, baking soda, and baking powder.

STEP 3: Large Bowl; Whisk; Rubber Spatula

Melt butter in microwave. Mix together butter and oil. Add eggs and egg whites. Mix well. Add yogurt, vanilla, sugar, and 1 tsp powdered coffee.

STEP 4: Small Bowl; Whisk; Rubber Spatula; Microwave

Melt chocolate. Add to batter. Add dry ingredients. Mix.

STEP 5: Oven; Toothpick; Potholders; Cooling Rack

Bake for 20 minutes. Check with toothpick. Cool on rack. Turn off oven.

STEP 6: Medium Bowl; Electric Mixer; Knife

Mix powdered sugar, cream cheese, 1 tsp powdered coffee, and vanilla until creamy. Put on cupcakes.

2013
Mini Cheesecakes

Tools

 Measuring Spoons	 Dry & Liquid Measuring Cups	 Oven	 Potholders	 Spoon	
 Electric Mixer	 Knives	 Cutting Board	 Bowl	Mini Muffin Tin	 Cooling Rack

Ingredients

 cooking spray	 20 square wonton wrappers	 8 oz less-fat cream cheese	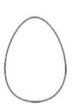 1 egg	 ½ cup sugar	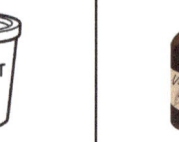 2 Tbsp fat-free yogurt
½ tsp vanilla					

1 Tbsp wheat flour

Topping Options: Sliced Berries, Maple Syrup, Shredded Coconut, Sliced Almonds

32

Directions

STEP 1: Oven; Mini Muffin Tins

Preheat oven to 350°F. Spray 20 mini muffin cups with <u>cooking spray</u>. Press a <u>wonton wrapper</u> into each muffin cup.

STEP 2: Bowl; Electric Mixer; Measuring Spoons; Dry & Liquid Measuring Cups

Beat together <u>cream cheese</u>, <u>egg</u>, <u>sugar</u>, <u>yogurt</u>, <u>flour</u>, and <u>vanilla</u> until smooth and creamy.

STEP 3: Spoon

Spoon equal amount of mixture into each lined cup.

STEP 4: Oven; Potholders; Cooling Rack

Bake 16 to 18 minutes (wrappers are browned and filling is set). Set on cooling rack. Let cool before removing from tins. Turn oven off.

STEP 5:

Optional: Add <u>toppings</u>.

2014
Biscotti

Tools

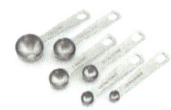 Measuring Spoons	 Dry Measuring Cups	 Oven	 Potholders

 Knives	 Electric Mixer	 Bowl	 Water	 Baking Sheet	 Cooling Rack

Ingredients

 cooking spray	 6 Tbsp butter	 ⅔ cup sugar	 1 ½ tsp baking powder	 1 tsp cinnamon	 ¼ tsp salt	 1 tsp vanilla

 2 eggs	 1 ¾ cup wheat flour	 ½ cup rolled oats	 ½ cup nuts	 cinnamon sugar (1 Tbsp cinnamon + 1/4 cup sugar)

Directions

STEP 1: Oven; Baking Sheet

Preheat oven to 350°F. Spray baking sheet with cooking spray.

STEP 2: Bowl; Electric Mixer; Dry Measuring Cups; Measuring Spoons

Beat together butter, sugar, baking powder, cinnamon, salt, and vanilla until smooth. Add eggs. Mix well. Add wheat flour and oats. Mix again. Stir in nuts.

STEP 3: Baking Sheet

Divide dough into 4 equal pieces. Place them on baking sheet. Shape each piece into a rough log. Line them 2 inches apart. Using damp hands, flatten and smooth logs until they are ¾ inch thick. Rub tops with a little bit of water and sprinkle with cinnamon-sugar.

STEP 4: Oven; Potholders; Cooling Rack; Knife: Baking Sheet

Bake 23 to 25 minutes. Allow them to cool on pan for 10 minutes. Rub tops with more water, sprinkle more cinnamon-sugar. Cool for 15 to 20 more minutes. Reduce oven temperature to 325°F. Cut logs crosswise into ½ inch slices. Place back on baking sheet. Bake for 25 minutes. Remove from oven and cool on the pan. Turn oven off.

2015
Fudgy Black Bean Brownies

Tools

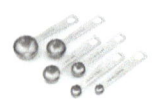 Measuring Spoons	 Dry & Liquid Measuring Cup	 Oven	 Potholders	 Rubber Spatula
 8X8 Baking Dish	 Food Processor	 Strainer	 Toothpick	 Cooling Rack

Ingredients

 cooking spray	 1 can (15 oz) black beans	 3 eggs	 3 Tbsp canola oil	 ¾ cup sugar
 ½ cocoa powder	 1 tsp vanilla	 ½ tsp baking powder	 ¼ tsp salt	 ½ cup mini semi-sweet chocolate chips

Directions

STEP 1: Oven; Baking Dish

Preheat oven to 350°F. Spray baking dish with cooking spray.

STEP 2: Strainer

Strain and rinse black beans.

STEP 3: Food Processor; Measuring Spoons; Dry & Liquid Measuring Cups

Put black beans in the bowl of food processor. Pulse until smooth. Add eggs, oil, sugar, cocoa powder, vanilla, baking powder, and salt. Process until smooth. Add ¼ cup of chocolate chips. Pulse until mixed.

STEP 4: Baking Dish; Rubber Spatula

Pour batter into prepared pan. Sprinkle with the remaining chocolate chips.

STEP 5: Oven; Toothpick; Potholders; Cooling Rack

Bake 30 to 35 minutes. Check with toothpick. Turn oven off. Cool in pan before slicing into 2-inch squares.

2016
Blueberry Lemon Yogurt Cake

Tools

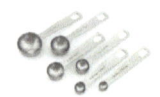 Measuring Spoons	 Dry & Liquid Measuring Cup	 Oven	 Potholders	 Utensils
 Bowls	 Loaf Pan	 Grater	 Microwave	 Toothpick	 Cooling Rack

Ingredients

 cooking spray	 1 ½ cups wheat flour	 2 tsp baking powder	 ½ tsp salt	 ¾ cup non-fat yogurt	 ⅔ cup sugar
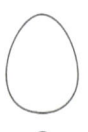 3 eggs	 ½ tsp vanilla	 ½ cup olive oil	 2 lemons (2 Tbsp juice & 1 Tbsp zest)	 1 cup fresh or frozen blueberries	 2 tsp honey

Directions

STEP 1: Oven; Loaf Pan

Preheat oven to 325°F. Lightly spray loaf pan with <u>cooking spray</u>.

STEP 2: Bowl; Whisk; Dry Measuring Cups; Measuring Spoons

Whisk together <u>wheat flour</u>, <u>baking powder</u>, and <u>salt</u>.

STEP 3: Bowl; Grater; Dry & Liquid Measuring Cups; Measuring Spoons; Whisk; Rubber Spatula

Pour <u>sugar</u> into second bowl. Use grater to get <u>lemon zest</u>. Rub <u>lemon zest</u> into <u>sugar</u> until yellow and fragrant. Add <u>yogurt</u>, <u>eggs</u>, and <u>vanilla</u>. Whisk well. Slowly whisk in <u>dry ingredients</u>. With spatula, fold in the <u>oil</u>.

STEP 4: Small Bowl; Dry Measuring Cups; Measuring Spoons; Rubber Spatula

Toss <u>blueberries</u> in <u>1 teaspoon flour</u>. Gently fold <u>blueberries</u> into <u>batter</u>.

STEP 5: Loaf Pan; Oven; Potholders; Cooling Rack

Pour <u>batter</u> into pan. Bake 50 to 55 minutes. Check with toothpick. Let cool in pan for 30 minutes. Turn oven off. Juice the <u>lemons</u>. Warm <u>2 Tbsp lemon juice</u> and <u>2 tsp honey</u>. Whisk. Brush <u>glaze</u> on warm cake. Remove cake carefully. Cool, slice, and serve.

2017
Blueberry Baked Oatmeal

Tools

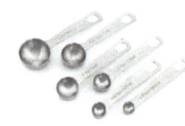 Measuring Spoons	  Dry & Liquid Measuring Cup	 Oven
 Potholders	 Whisk	 Bowls	 9-inch Baking Dish	Cooling Rack

Ingredients

 cooking spray	 2 cups rolled oats	 2 tsp cinnamon	 1 tsp baking powder	 ½ tsp salt	¼ tsp nutmeg	 1 ¾ cups skim milk
 ¼ cup maple syrup	 2 eggs	 1 Tbsp + 1 tsp butter	 2 tsp vanilla		 2 ½ cups fresh or frozen blueberries	 1 tsp sugar

Directions

STEP 1: Oven; Baking Dish

Preheat oven to 375°F. Spray baking dish with cooking spray.

STEP 2: Medium Bowl; Whisk; Dry Measuring Cups; Measuring Spoons

Whisk together oats, cinnamon, baking powder, salt, and nutmeg.

STEP 3: Small Bowl; Liquid Measuring Cups; Measuring Spoons; Whisk

Combine milk, maple syrup, eggs, butter, and vanilla. Mix.

STEP 4: Baking Dish; Dry Measuring Cup

Arrange 2 cups of berries on bottom of baking dish. Cover fruit with dry oat mixture. Drizzle wet ingredients over oats. Gentle shake baking dish to spread wet ingredients. Make sure all oats are soaked. Scatter the remaining berries on top. Sprinkle with raw sugar.

STEP 5: Oven; Potholders; Cooling Rack

Bake 42 to 47 minutes. Remove from oven. Turn oven off. Let cool for 5 minutes before serving.

2018
Mug Cakes (Vanilla and Chocolate)

Tools

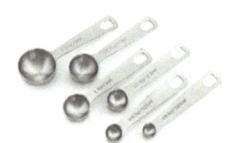 Measuring Spoons	 Fork	 Small Bowls	 Large Mug	 Microwave

Ingredients

Vanilla Cake:	 cooking spray	 2 Tbsp wheat flour	 1 Tbsp sugar	 ¼ tsp baking powder	 pinch salt	 1 tsp canola oil	 2 Tbsp milk	 ¼ tsp vanilla
For Chocolate Cake, add:				 2 tsp cocoa powder			 1 tsp mini chocolate chips	
Frosting for Two:	 3 Tbsp powdered sugar		 1 tsp softened butter			 1 Tbsp milk		 ¼ tsp vanilla

Directions

Vanilla Mug Cake

Small Bowl #1; Measuring Spoons; Fork; Large Mug; Microwave

Spray mug with cooking spray. Add wheat flour, sugar, baking powder, and salt into mug. Whisk with fork. Add oil, milk, and vanilla. Stir well. Microwave for 60 seconds.

Chocolate Mug Cake

Small Bowl #1; Measuring Spoons; Fork; Large Mug; Microwave

Spray mug with cooking spray. Add wheat flour, sugar, cocoa powder, baking powder, and salt into mug. Whisk with fork. Add oil, milk, and vanilla. Stir well. Fold in chocolate chips. Microwave for 60 seconds.

Frosting for Two

Small Bowl; Fork

Mix all ingredients together. Drizzle over cake.

Dietary Accommodations

Dairy Free
Affected Pages: 6-7, 10-11, 18-19, 24-35, 38-43

Butter: Applesauce; mashed bananas; mashed avocado; vegetable oil; dairy-free labeled butter

Buttermilk: Any type of dairy-free milk (e.g. soy, almond, coconut) + 1 Tbsp lemon juice

Cheese/Goat Cheese: Dairy-free labeled cheeses; nutritional yeast

Chocolate: Dairy-free labeled chocolate

Cream Cheese: Dairy-free labeled cream cheese; coconut milk; tofu/tofu spread

Skim Milk: Any type of dairy-free milk

Yogurt: Dairy-free buttermilk (see above); almond milk yogurt; pureed tofu

Gluten Free
Affected Pages: 6-11, 16-21, 24-33, 36-37, 42-43

Wheat Wraps/Hamburger Buns: Large pieces of lettuce; corn tortillas

Bread Crumbs: Fine oats (run in food processor); flax or fiber cereal

Flour: Cornmeal; gluten-free labeled flour (e.g. almond, coconut, rice, buckwheat)

Pizza Dough: Cauliflower pizza crust; Portobello mushroom caps; quinoa pizza crust

Wonton Wrappers: Gluten-free labeled wonton wrappers; homemade with gluten-free flour

Dietary Accommodations

Vegan Substitutes
Affected Pages: 6-11, 16-19, 24-43

Butter: Applesauce; mashed bananas; mashed avocado; vegetable oil; vegan butter

Butter/Skim Milk: Any type of dairy-free milk (e.g. soy, coconut) + 1 Tbsp lemon juice

Cheese/Goat Cheese: Dairy-free labeled cheeses; nutritional yeast

Chocolate: Dairy-free labeled chocolate

Cream Cheese: Dairy-free labeled cream cheese; coconut milk; tofu/tofu spread

Eggs: Silken tofu; applesauce; mashed banana; arrowroot powder

Yogurt: Dairy-free buttermilk (see above); almond milk yogurt; pureed tofu

Food Selectivity

'Picky eating,' or food selectivity, is an eating disorder that often worries parents. Nearly half of children are picky eaters. It is common among children with autism and Attention Deficit Hyperactivity Disorder (ADHD). Children with food selectivity often eat less than 10 different foods. They also struggle trying new foods. Picky eaters tend to eat things like yogurt, juice, peanut butter, bread, and cereal. All of these foods contain artificial food coloring. Artificial food coloring reduces the nutritional content of the foods children eat. This cookbook introduces healthier versions of familiar foods (e.g. burgers and cookies). This cookbook is child friendly. Invite the child to cook/bake alongside you. This has been shown to increase the chances of a child trying new foods.

Nutrition Information: Sargent Choice Recipes

All recipes are available online at bu.edu/scnc/category/sctk/

Autumn Coffee Cake (Blog Post: Bianca Tamburello)
Calories 200 | Fat 9 g | Sat. Fat 1 g | Carbs 28 g | Fiber 3 g | Protein 4 g

Biscotti (Blog Post: Stephanie Smith)
Calories 160 | Fat 5 g | Sat. Fat 3 g | Carbs 24 g | Fiber 1 g | Protein 4 g

Black Bean Burgers (Blog Post: Bianca Tamburello)

Blueberry Baked Oatmeal (Blog Post: Jay Patruno; Adapted from Cookie and Kate)
Calories 260 | Sat. Fat 2 g | Carbs 40 g | Fiber 5 g | Protein 9 g | Sodium 330 mg

Blueberry Lemon Yogurt Cake (Blog Post: Alaina Coffey; Adapted from Cookie and Kate) Calories 220 | Fat 12 g | Sat. Fat 2 g | Carbs 27 g | Fiber 2 g | Protein 4 g

Brown Rice Sushi (Blog Post: Caroline Patrick)
Calories 250 | Fat 10 g | Sat. Fat 1.5 g | Carbs 28 g | Fiber 6 g | Protein 12 g

Caramelized Onion and Goat Cheese Pizza (Blog Post: Rachel Priebe)

Fudgy Black Bean Brownies (Blog Post: Rachel Priebe; Recipe from Meal Makeover Mom's cookbook, No Whine with Dinner)

Kale and White Bean Potpie with Chive Biscuits (Blog Post: Jay Patruno; Recipe from Eating Well)

Karen's Beloved Potato Latkes (Blog Post: Bianca Tamburello)
Calories 360 | Fat 15 g | Sat. Fat 2.5 g | Carbs 54 g | Fiber 7 g | Protein 5 g

Mini Cheesecakes (Blog Post: Rachel Priebe; Recipe from Meal Makeover Mom's Cookbook, No Whine with Dinner)

Nutrition Information: Sargent Choice Recipes

Mocha Cupcakes with Mocha Cream Cheese Frosting (Blog Post: Bianca Tamburello; Adapted from Ellie Krieger, The Food You Crave)
Calories 140 | Fat 7 g | Sat. Fat 3 g | Carbs 18 g | Fiber 2 g | Protein 4 g

Mug Cakes (Blog Post: Caroline Kohler; Adapted from https://bitzngiggles.com and Café Delites)

Oven-Baked Vegetable Burritos with Cheese (Blog Post: Bianca Tamburello)
Calories 480 | Fat 13 g | Sat. Fat 5 g | Carbs 68 g | Protein 23 g

Pumpkin Cranberry Muffins (Blog Post: Bianca Tamburello; Adapted from Cooking Light, Nov. 2007) Calories 180 | Fat 3 g | Carbs 39 g | Fiber 3 g | Protein 3 g

Roasted Root Vegetables with Rosemary (Blog Post: Alaina Coffey; From Bon Appétit Magazine) Calories 270 | Fat 11 g | Sat. Fat 1.5 g | Carbs 42 g | Fiber 9 g | Protein 5 g | Sodium 420 mg

Shredded Jackfruit Burritos (Blog Post: Caroline Kohler; Adapted from https://101cookbooks.com)

Southwestern Corn and Black Bean Salad (Blog Post: Tre Pina) Calories 160 | Fat 4.5 g | Sat. Fat 1 g | Carbs 29 g | Fiber 7 g | Protein 8 g | Sodium 170 mg

Spicy Lentils with Sweet Potatoes and Kale (Blog Post: Rachel Priebe; Adapted from Eat Live Run Blog) Calories 370 | Fat 14 g | Sat. Fat 3.5 g | Carbs 48 g | Fiber 8 g | Protein 14 g | Sodium 380 mg

Whole Grain Peanut Butter Chocolate Chip Cookies
Calories 125 | Fat 8 g | Sat. Fat 2 g | Carbs 13 g | Fiber 1 g | Protein 3 g

About This Cookbook

All clipart or recipe images are royalty free or from the Sargent Choice Test Kitchen blog.

All recipes and information used in this cookbook have been scanned through a readability feature to ensure the language is at or below a 5th grade reading level, to support English as a Second Language speakers, individuals with disabilities, and children of various ages.

All font sizes are size 16 or bigger to support individuals who have low vision or other vision impairments.

We have shared our favorite savory recipes from the Sargent Choice Test Kitchen. Now it is your turn.

Write your favorite savory recipe here!

Title: _____

Tools

_____
_____
_____

Ingredients

_____
_____
_____

Directions

_____
_____
_____
_____

We have shared our favorite sweet recipes from the Sargent Choice Test Kitchen. Now it is your turn.

Write your favorite sweet recipe here!

Title: _____

Tools

_____
_____
_____

Ingredients

_____
_____
_____

Directions

_____
_____
_____
_____
_____

About Us

MEGAN BARTLEY is an occupational therapy doctoral student at Boston University. She has been baking with her mom and grandmothers since she could hold a spoon. Megan thoroughly enjoys "kitchen karaoke." She founded and hosts Recipe for Life, a baking exploration group for international students, and is the owner of Blessed Mess Baked Goods, a donation-based baking business. She can be reached at mbartley@bu.edu

KATIE HAY is a visual artist and writer who loves making food, eating food, and sharing meals with others. As a Creative Writing, MSc candidate at the University of Edinburgh, she hopes to write and illustrate fiction works that invite young people and families to live life more fully and lovingly. She can be reached at haykatie14@gmail.com; see more of her work at www.hay210.com

KAREN JACOBS is an occupational therapist, an ergonomist and a Clinical Professor in the Department of Occupational Therapy at Boston University. Karen is an Amma (grandma in Icelandic) to four grandchildren. She is the founder and host of the Sargent Choice Test Kitchen where students trial the Sargent Choice recipes. Karen can be reached at kjacobs@bu.edu

www.ingramcontent.com/pod-product-compliance
Lightning Source LLC
Chambersburg PA
CBHW041434010526
44118CB00002B/72